Railways & R...
GOTHERINGTON
The story of a station reborn
1981-2010

Bryan Nicholls

The original GWR station at Gotherington was opened in 1906 and closed in 1955. This is the story from 1981, when we purchased the premises, until the present day – a resurrection...

Contents

Acknowledgments

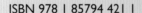

© Bryan Nicholls 2012

Photographs: © Bryan and Savita

First published in 2012

British Library Cataloguing in Publication Data
A catalogue record for this book is available from the British Library

Printed and bound in Ceská Republika

ISBN 978 1 85794 421 1

Silver Link Publishing Ltd
The Trundle
Ringstead Road
Great Addington
Kettering
Northants NN14 4BW

Tel/Fax: 01536 330588
email: sales@nostalgiacollection.com
Website: www.nostalgiacollection.com

Thanks to all those who were positive in the belief that this could be done, and your help when required is not forgotten. Special thanks must go to Savita for the painstaking process of collating the text and images using the IT skills that I do not possess. It must also be obvious that the tremendous floral displays as witnessed by the passing trains are a result of her dedication.

Above right: Gotherington station In August 1981.

Right: The station in its heyday, from a painting by Joe Wilkes.

Far right: This 1981 photograph clearly shows the modern extension, which we did not build.

Introduction

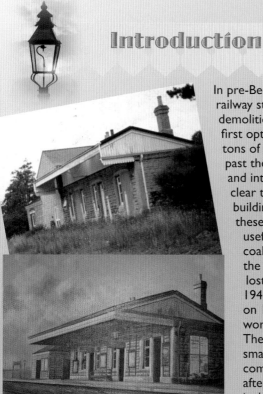

In pre-Beeching days, when a railway station had closed instant demolition was not always the first option. With hundreds of tons of pulsating steel hammering past the windows every day and into the night, it was quite clear that very substantial buildings were required and these early closures found a useful afterlife as farm stores, coal merchants, offices and the like. Gotherington had lost its station master in 1941 and closed completely on 13 June 1955 after a working life of just 49 years. The down platform with its small waiting shelter was completely demolished soon after, but as luck would have it the main buildings on the up side were rented out by British Railways to a former employee as living quarters. The goods yard had closed in 1949 and the rails lifted immediately, leaving a large area to return very quickly to nature. In the midst of this rural idyll the new tenant, surrounded by free-range hens, took to slaughtering them in the goods shed, which incidentally, after a quick wipe over with a damp rag, now serves as our dining room.

The whole railway complex here at Gotherington began a downward spiral as BR, in an effort to avoid maintenance costs, removed the remaining platform and viciously hacked off the front of the canopy, leaving an odd gaping hole in the roof space. The freehold on the entire site was bought in 1978 by a man intent on expanding it into a large family home. Regrettably all remaining railway features were disposed of, including the large sliding doors of the goods shed, spear-topped iron railings and nameboard posts, leaving very few clues as to the site's original function.

What came next was a defining moment in the history of Gotherington station, for it would never look quite the same again. When constructed by the Great Western Railway in 1905 the chosen medium for the single-storey building was stone blocks from the nearby Cleeve quarry, giving the walls a thickness of nearly 24 inches. A small detached goods shed of similar construction was built about 30 feet away to the west. The new owner decided to bridge the gap between the two with a modern-looking two-storey addition, which forms the main living quarters of the building that you see today. The following story tells how we built a brand-new Gotherington station from the ashes of the old.

THE BIG FOUR?

BRYAN NICHOLLS 'I was born in Gloucester, spent most of my working life in the music industry, and have had a life-long interest in railways. Savita and I bought the premises at Gotherington in 1981.'

SAVITA 'Having spent most of my early life living in the centre of Cheltenham, in 1981 my knowledge of rural life was rather spartan and my knowledge of railway history even less. Hence I had a steep learning curve. Skills I had never encountered were acquired and swiftly implemented. The many varied and complex challenges of rural railway life have required great stamina, determination and commitment.

 The last 30 years have been a truly unique experience and now, as I look around the various nooks and crannies of the station, I realise what a worthwhile endeavour it's all been and thanks must go to Bryan for his inspiration, vision and total commitment to creating what some would consider a rather unusual home!'

Far left: **JACK MORTIMER** (1913-2004), photographed at Withington station, helped not only to build the platforms at Gotherington but gave sterling service on most of the major projects here until 1988.

Left: **WILL** at work on the bay platform. We encountered Will in 1996, and he gave me the opportunity to expand beyond my initial expectations and was responsible for creating some iconic structures here. Three huge level crossing gates, the loading gauge and the ground frame building are just a few examples of his work. The Gotherington West branch would simply have not been possible without his particular skills.

Above: The author in the workshop at Gotherington.

Right: Gotherington and Savita in bloom in June 2010.

By the spring of 1981 my penchant for collecting worthless bits of scrap metal from the steam age meant that living in a tiny Cheltenham town house became impractical. Early indications of this were largely ignored, but the realisation that a clenched fist could be placed between the skirting board and floor of an upstairs room gave the game away – this was heavy stuff.

I was born and raised in Gloucester within the sounds and smells of Horton Road loco shed, so I quite fancied returning to the lineside if at all possible. Several Sunday afternoon forays into the beautiful Gloucestershire countryside were undertaken in the hope that something suitable would catch our eye. It was while speeding homewards from one such expedition that the tall stone chimney stacks of an elongated, tin-roofed building were glimpsed briefly between the wavering 75-year-old Scots pine trees to the east of Gotherington village. As GWR historians will be eager to tell you, 'pines means lines'. The GWR would usually plant a row or two of these lofty, quick-growing trees adjacent to each newly constructed station, supposedly to placate landowners subjected to compulsory purchase of their properties and who in many cases considered the presence of the railway as an eyesore! Former station sites can still be identified, long after closure and demolition, due to the 100-year lifespan of the Scots pine. Remembering all of this meant that further investigation was necessary. A gap in the hedgerow on Granna Lane provided a much clearer view and, to our utter amazement, we were indeed faced with the sorry remains of the former railway station; it appeared that some new building work on the site meant an end to it ever resembling railway premises again. We drove away saddened at this prospect, but vowed to continue our search for a new home with local railway connections.

What followed could be viewed as pure serendipity, or maybe even karma to those who believe, but the facts are thus. You may recall that our discovery of the Gotherington site came on a Sunday afternoon, so can you imagine our total disbelief in finding those premises advertised for sale in the local paper the very next day! Ignoring the usual requisite protocol, we bundled ourselves into the car and drove headlong out to investigate further. Opting to use the original GWR station approach road, we passed the two delightful stone cottages built for the porter and signalman, then the large detached station master's house on our right. At this time all of these beautiful buildings were in their original unaltered state. At the head of the drive stood the former station building and goods shed, now linked together by the modern extension.

Fuelled by an adrenaline flow, I hammered on the only visible door and engaged in discussion with the owner. After a tour of the land and buildings offered for sale, I resolved to stem the tide of change and possibly even to reverse some of the recent 'improvements'. Blissfully unaware of what lay ahead for us, the epoch-making decision to buy the property was taken. So while the entire nation was celebrating the national holiday awarded for the Royal Wedding of Charles and Diana, we could be found amid dozens of tea chests and cardboard boxes contemplating a very different future.

THIS IS WHAT WE BOUGHT

The station is seen on 12 August 1981 with no platforms, a gaping hole in the canopy and clearly showing the modern extension built by its previous owner.

THE WORK BEGINS

Saturday 1 August 1981 was very hot indeed and not conducive to hard physical toil, but we now owned an empty former railway station and set about filling it up. We are rather proud of the fact that after many dozens of journeys from both Gloucester and Cheltenham using a borrowed, battered blue Transit van, the only damage sustained was to a couple of my old shellac 78rpm records. Surrounded by hungry chickens, an overflowing septic tank, no proper cooking facilities and all our worldly possessions stacked to the ceiling, we flopped into two borrowed armchairs and turned on a small portable TV set. Nothing could have been more aptly titled as we watched Boris Karloff in *Bedlam*. Four evenings later a violent electric storm knocked off the power supply and left me scrambling for candles. I remember feeling both anger and fear in equal measure, but luckily a good friend of mine came round with several bottles of excellent red wine to lift my spirits. We lit a fire, watched the exaggerated shadows dance on the high bare walls of the lounge, and stayed up all night discussing what I wished to achieve at Gotherington. A few very informative days were spent in the reference library at Gloucester where a little of the history surrounding the railway was gleaned but, more importantly, a small selection of photographs came to light.

Following a meeting with the original directors of the Gloucestershire Warwickshire Railway, who had just set up their headquarters at Toddington, it was agreed that if it was entirely at my own expense I could rebuild not only our up-side platform but also the former down platform, which had existed on land that the G/WR now owned. Elated at this prospect I returned home to where the true immensity of the task ahead became crystal clear. I had never laid a brick in my life, and a rough calculation seemed to suggest that around 30,000 were needed for the first platform alone! The first of these problems was easily solved as my retired uncle had spent more than 30 years as a civil engineer on British Railways Western Region and at 70 years of age was 'up for it'.

The brick question amazingly sorted itself soon afterwards as we came to realise that at some stage the original up platform, dating from 1905, had been simply bulldozed backwards onto land that we now owned. Hidden under a thick layer of topsoil were the many thousands of blue engineering bricks needed for the rebuild. The late summer evenings were taken up with the excavation and cleaning of enough of these to start on the first section – but where to start?

It seemed logical to try to locate the original Edwardian footings, so a series of test holes were dug by hand before discovering the solid red-brick base some 2 feet below the ballast. The Great Western Railway platforms here had been 400 feet long, but a decision was taken to limit these to a more realistic length of 200 feet. Even so, the next job of shovelling away by hand tons of ballast to expose that amount of the footings required a certain chain-gang mentality, and a knowledge of the Paul Robeson song catalogue helped things along.

The first bricks were laid in November, but time was divided between this outside project and renewing floor joists inside the former ladies waiting room, which was to be our kitchen. Many weeks behind schedule, the kitchen still lacked a sink and was only completed in early December after a chaotic three-month period of installation. Imagine then our sheer joy just two weeks later when early one morning outside the window a beautiful winter scene presented itself. Down came the snow, followed unfortunately by half of the kitchen ceiling… The newly purchased wheelbarrow was swiftly emptied of blue bricks and brought inside to catch the torrent of

water cascading from burst pipes in the station loft. We foolishly thought that the lounge would offer us more protection, but just minutes later we saw the TV disappear under a waterfall!

Until a plumber arrived we made coffee by boiling snow in a kettle over a log fire. Nearly 30 separate fractures were eventually found in the plumbing system, and we decided that priority must be given to providing an adequate heating system for the entire property. Just seven days later on Sunday 20 December 1981 came the moment that would have sent lesser mortals running back to the comfort and safety of a small house in town. Gale-force winds ripped out eight glass panels from the station canopy and sent them into orbit like magic carpets around the chimney stacks. Most of them ended upright in the front garden and, bearing in mind that they measured 8 feet by 2 feet, it appeared that we'd had a garden make-over with futuristic sculptures, in advance of this becoming de rigueur a decade later.

1982 continued to excite and inspire. On 8 January, after a company meeting in Birmingham, I left to drive home in 8 inches of snow. The 55-mile journey took more than 5 hours and I eventually had to abandon my car on a main road and trek home to the station. Waist-high drifts greeted me as I tried to thrash a route to the front door with my bare hands. The following morning I woke to find

Left: The station approach, snowed in during our first winter.

Above: Work begins on the up platform, 1 November 1981. Jack Mortimer finds the original 1905 GWR footings to begin laying bricks for our new platforms.

Right: Having built the first section of retaining wall, the coping stones are man-handled into place on 6 December 1981.

myself totally cut off from the rest of civilisation. Snow had engulfed the whole single-storey building, trapping me inside and alone with just a few small logs for the fire, an empty Calor gas cylinder, no running water and very little food left. Rescue came two days later when friends carved a 'canyon' through the snowdrift, but the person answering the door to them was not the gaunt emaciated figure they had expected. Emerging from the gloom and wearing most of the contents of my wardrobe I must have looked like a mummified Michelin man. At minus 21 degrees we all knew what

Right: Under snow, 12 December 1981.

Below: Jack fixes the newly acquired valance boards from the Frome station bonfire while Savita is busy stripping down the interior doors that divided the booking office from the ladies waiting room. Very soon the new platform retaining wall would appear on the right of the picture.

would happen next, and as soon as the ice on the inside walls of the old booking office began to melt it was time to get into Gene Kelly mode. This time the bedrooms benefited from a wash down as water oozed from the electric light fittings before turning the bookcases downstairs into a nice little indoor water feature. Suffice to say it was all character-building stuff but set us back many weeks, having to remove ceilings, rewire the building, renew carpets, install an indoor stop-tap and re-plumb yet again. If we could withstand all of this…

Bricklaying had resumed in earnest by February, with time off for good behaviour to visit the railway works in Swindon, Derby and Doncaster at a time when permits were available to do so. Progress was such that by April the first half of the platform retaining wall was complete and awaited the large coping stones I had obtained from the now closed BR engineers department in Gloucester. This yard contained redundant railway material and I was lucky enough to purchase a pair of level crossing gates, two large cast-iron GWR lamps and nearly enough coping stones to complete the platform, and still get change from £50 (including delivery). A similar yard at Ashton Gate in Bristol provided the new front section valance boards for Gotherington station. These 100-year-old wooden shapes had been taken down from the canopy extension of Frome station in Somerset, and just days before I had discovered them piled high and about to be burned.

'Can I buy your bonfire?' I enquired.

'If you can stretch to 25 pence,' was the reply, and I was issued with a receipt for 'firewood'. Such was the bargain-bin nature of certain large railway artefacts in those days, and as it dawned on me that there was a lot of empty space to fill at Gotherington, perhaps a plan needed to be drawn up to recover as much as possible. Within just a few weeks that plan had turned into a full-scale military-style operation.

Merthyr goods yard, before the incident…

My work took me into South and West Wales so, armed with a map showing the routes of long-closed lines and stations, I systematically scoured each line in turn over the next six years. Each time an item was discovered an offer was made for it to the British Rail stores controller at Reading, who then issued a permit to remove it. It usually worked like clockwork and, with a very cheaply hired lorry, we would set off armed with picks, shovels and unbridled enthusiasm. Occasionally setbacks occurred, such as the infamous Merthyr incident. We had fought successfully against the odds to remove a large cast-iron GWR lamp standard from the old goods yard at Merthyr Tydfil. By the time this lumbering beast had been manhandled onto the back of the lorry to join the rest of the day's spoils we were more than happy to hit the homeward trail. Sadly our driver must have misheard my instructions that Saturday afternoon as all we hit was a jagged rail, slashing a tyre to ribbons. Seemingly stranded after many fruitless phone calls for assistance (there was no spare tyre), we resolved to spend the night in the rubbish-strewn railway yard. Remarkably, while kicking our heels amid the clutter, some 4 hours later

Above: Jack at work on the first section of the up platform, 11 November 1981.

Left: Snow stops work in December 1981.

an old discarded wheel hub with tyre came to light. It was flat, it was gouged, it was awful, but it fitted and it got us home safely in the early hours of Sunday morning.

Film buffs may wish to remember 12 August 1982 as the day that Hollywood legend Henry Fonda passed away. However, on that very same day, some 5,000 miles east of Los Angeles, the village of Gotherington regained one of its railway platforms. Well, almost…

The last brick had been laid in the retaining wall and the heavy coping stones bedded on top, but this left an enormous pit to fill up behind the wall. Acting swiftly, I arranged for the 'diversion' of several large tipper lorries carrying brick rubble from demolished riding stables at nearby Gretton. The drivers were more than happy to dump their loads locally, but the downside for us was a back garden resembling the East End of London after the blitz.

For a number of reasons it was not possible to move most of this mess by mechanical means, so over the next few weeks, as time and energy allowed, the trusty wheelbarrow was put to good use. Anyone who has laid a patio will appreciate that the hardcore base has to be compacted firmly, and we were about to lay a 'patio' on the grand scale, so lots of bashing and stomping then took place.

GWR station platforms were surfaced in a number of different ways and one of the most delightful to my mind utilised flat blue engineering bricks sporting a small non-slip diamond tread pattern. On a recent Welsh expedition I had purchased the remains of Pontypool Crane Street station platforms. After removing, with some difficulty, the two large cast-iron lamp standards engulfed by mature trees, I remembered that buried deep in the undergrowth here were many hundreds of these

Above: The up platform – a big hole to fill by summer 1982.

Left: Rubble for the platform backfill.

durable bricks. It was just a few miles down the road from where I worked mid-week in those days, so Wednesday evenings would see me scrabbling about on all fours in the bushes with a jemmy, lifting as many bricks as would fit into the back of my estate car. Trips back home up the M50 would be made with the car pointing skywards at 45 degrees.

Things went well for a few weeks until the long arm of the law, which had been monitoring my excavations, reached out one chilly night and yanked me across to the nearby police station for questioning. Written proof that I wasn't the phantom station stealer lay on my desk 100 miles away, and without this BR receipt for £10 I had a little difficulty in proving that the town's 130-year-old platform was being moved to Gloucestershire in the back of a Ford Cortina. Common sense prevailed eventually, and the second half of Platform 1 at Gotherington was finished in the more usual large-format concrete slabs. A number of these came from a neighbour's garden and are the 1906 GWR originals.

Although now unmistakably looking like a railway station again, the overall appearance was still one of abandonment and the new platform needed to be brought to life. A short list of essentials was quickly drawn up and it was off to plunder the valleys again. Three cast-iron lamp standards were dug out of Cardiff's Ninian Park Halt, much to the amusement of the crew aboard diesel loco No 37294, which passed through with a rake of rusty 20-ton hoppers. In those days it was normal practice for BR to just smash to pieces any redundant material that was not easily removable, but we loved a challenge and a 6-foot-high metal fence did not stop us claiming our booty. Other similar heavy lamps were found in situ at Ammanford, Ogmore Vale, Pontypool Road and Brynmenyn. At this last location we were mistaken for BR employees by a kindly old lady who brought us a pot of tea on a silver tray and thanked us for finally removing the 'eyesores' outside her cottage adjacent to the level crossing. Once again, though, the good folk of Pontypool weren't so trusting and (suspecting nefarious

activity) called the police as we dug out the sole remaining lamp on Pontypool Road station approach. An off-duty plain-clothes officer arrived and wasn't too pleased that he had been called away from the pub to deal with the situation. I hastily fumbled in my pockets for one of the official permits and mistakenly gave him a completely unrelated document. He smiled, said goodbye and went back to his entertainment.

The Great Western Railway used a very specific design for the weighty cast-iron columns that supported the nameboards on its stations. I needed a matching pair for Gotherington and found the ideal candidates on the platform of the long-closed Llangeinor station at the foot of the Garw valley. The station house here was still occupied and enquiries revealed that an elderly couple now owned the posts as part of their garden. Disbelief at my request to buy them was swiftly followed by an estimation of their worth. The cost became irrelevant over the next three days, as that's how long it took three of us to extract them from their position. The deep mud acted as a suction pump against the broad metal base plates, and as we were sandwiched between a railway line (which still carried freight traffic) and a fence, the only way out of the holes was upwards. This was very hard work indeed, and we found solace in inventing new swear words to ease the burden, but some of the old favourites offended our Methodist hosts to the point where the deal was very nearly called off! The feeling of sheer joy on

Left: The lamps, the fence and the waiting car at Ninian Park Halt, Cardiff.

Above and right: Removing the nameboard posts at Llangeinor, 23 May 1983.

Above: Removing the spear-topped railings from Ross-on-Wye prior to the trailer puncture, 20 June 1989.

finally arriving home with both posts intact was cruelly shattered as one of them snapped in half as we unloaded, our lorry having got stuck in the loose ballast till rescued at 4.20am. To this day a slight kink can be seen in the repaired nameboard post, and it reminds me that it wasn't easy in those days but worth it in the end to save original pieces of our railway history.

The search was now on for the archetypal spear-headed metal fence panels once seen all over the former GWR system but now frowned upon by the current Health & Safety Executive. Purely by chance, on a visit to a friend in Ross-on-Wye, I caught a

glimpse of what looked like railings of this nature lining an alleyway alongside an electrical appliance shop. Pushing open the door to the alleyway I confirmed that at least ten panels of genuine GWR railings were there, albeit mostly buried beneath untamed undergrowth at the foot of the embankment carrying the former line to Hereford. A rather protracted deal was struck with the owners and we later dismantled the panels and loaded them onto a trailer for the journey back to their new home. They did eventually arrive at Gotherington but not before spending the night in a lay-by on the A40, as we blew a tyre on the trailer.

The long summer evenings of 1983 and 1984 saw me slowly removing everything I had paid British Railways for in South Wales. I came to realise that redevelopment would see the destruction of many railway locations and nothing should be

Above: My 12-seater Ford at Pantyffynon station yard on 27 June 1984!

branded station seat that was about to be cut to pieces.

Not all of the station furniture at Gotherington came from so far afield, however, and the splendid hand-cranked fire alarm seen fixed to the wall was discovered in the derelict GWR horse stables at Gloucester, together with half-a-dozen porter's sack trucks. My brother had constructed a 15-foot-long wooden replica nameboard, which when fitted between my sturdy supporting posts really proclaimed that at Gotherington a station was now back on the map.

I was foolish to ever believe that it could stop at this, and decisions taken in the ensuing weeks would dictate the pattern of my life for years to come.

Below: Bringing home a GWR bench from the miners welfare at Hafod-Yr-Ynys.

taken for granted, so with an almost paranoid fervour I would fill the car with anything railway-related that I could find. Cast-iron signs were still to be had if you looked hard enough, and I was amazed at the generosity of local people who would in some instances allow me to remove articles from their property for 'a packet of fags'.

Two lucky discoveries proved the urgency of my task. At Pantyffynon, a pub opposite the station was, that very night, about to light a huge bonfire on top of which balanced the 10-foot-long GWR wooden bench that graces our platform to this day. It was late in the day as I recall when we rescued this treasure from certain death by fire, and my car was already laden with a myriad of railway memorabilia, so it came up the M4 on the roof.

The GWR was not the only major railway company to enter South Wales, but there is little tangible evidence remaining of the LNWR's incursion into the valleys. Even in 1983 the passing motorists on the busy Heads of the Valleys road would be unaware that they had traversed the once remote junction at Nant-y-Bwch. Cars are fine for getting from A to B, but if you go for a walk it can be a voyage of discovery. From the back garden of a bungalow at Nant-y-Bwch I rescued an original LNWR

TOIL BY TORCHLIGHT!

The new platform looked OK, but to rebuild the corresponding, long-demolished one on the opposite side would really balance things up. Once again the back-breaking task of using a pick and shovel to locate footings began after work on Christmas Eve 1984. A sense of déjà vu prevailed as I toiled by torchlight to eventually expose a small enough length of red bricks to build upon. Not exactly at the top of my list of pleasant Christmas surprises the next day was the discovery of a small lake, gently rippling in the morning breeze, on top of those red bricks! The undulating beauty of the Cotswold escarpment has its downside, as water flowing from Nottingham Hill became a constant problem when building on this side of the trackbed. Blue bricks left over from building the first platform soon ran out, but luckily a local nursery had decided to

Left: The up platform in 1984 and (below) in 2009.

Right: The flooded footings of the down platform on Christmas Day 1984.

demolish its large brick-built seed sheds so a few thousand reds were salvaged for the back of the retaining wall. The speed with which this second platform was taking shape necessitated some smart thinking if we were not to grind to a halt through lack of materials. I needed one big hit and the obvious but not necessarily the easiest solution was to buy yet another platform and demolish it to provide enough bricks and edging stones to complete the job here.

On Sunday 20 October 1985 I drove to Purton for a photograph of *City of Truro* skirting the Severn estuary on a mystery rail tour from Gloucester. This was followed by lunch in the servants' hall at Clearwell Castle, a visit to the Dean Forest Railway and a trip to Withington to pay for the local station platforms that I had agreed to buy from the land owner the previous day. Our penchant for walking or cycling along closed railway routes had led us to discover the barely visible remains of both platforms from this M&SWJR station, closed in 1961. Mature trees had engulfed the whole site, making reclamation very difficult, but over an 18-month period enough bricks, stone blocks and those beautiful bull-nosed diamond-tread edging stones had made the journey back to Gotherington.

By July 1986 each brick had been handled six times, including cleaning, and the retaining wall stood aloft with yet another enormous chasm behind it, waiting to be

Above: Seen on 23 October 1985 is one of the Withington station platforms, both of which I purchased, demolished and moved to Gotherington.

Left: Jack is seen on 11 March 1986 using the blue engineering bricks from Withington to create the down platform now used by the Gloucestershire Warwickshire Railway.

filled. I arranged for the spoil from building work in Bishops Cleeve to be dumped onto our land and once again the wheelbarrow was employed to make the many thousands of journeys required to achieve a level compact surface. Mercifully this second platform was always going to be the poor relation of the two that my uncle and I had built here, as it required very little additional decoration apart from another gigantic nameboard and two more cast-iron support posts.

I firmly believe that attention to detail pays great dividends and, although the rescue of our first two posts was an exercise in madness, I wanted two more similar posts again this time. These were now becoming very hard to find, but I eventually located a redundant pair at the isolated Llangennech station on the Loughor estuary. Road access was poor here and my brother had to quickly design and construct a sturdy rolling chassis to transport them to firm loading ground before the ponderous eastward trek to Gloucestershire on a meandering, very low-slung trailer at 40mph.

Acquiring all these redundant bits and pieces was certainly very hard work in those days, but if one had the time and inclination the rewards for all the effort were tremendous. Almost without

exception, of course, redundant also meant neglected, maltreated or damaged. Most things that had so far been brought back to Gotherington had very little paint left on them, although interestingly the best-preserved paint scheme adorned the oldest item. This was a fluted cast-iron lamp standard removed from Undy, which sported the early GWR colours of light stone and maroon brown. It was obvious that an overall uniform livery must be adopted at Gotherington, not only to tidy things up but to give it some kind of identity. This was always going to be a contentious issue as certain railway enthusiasts are renowned for their pedantic attitude towards authenticity, especially, it seems, concerning the Great

Above and left: Removing the nameboard posts from the isolated station at Llangennech on 29 December 1986.

Western. I'm bound to say that I've a great deal of sympathy with this ideal and certainly I adhere to the maxim that 'if a job is worth doing…'

After a few false starts, I decided that my personal favourite appropriate colour scheme was from the period just after the Nationalisation of the railways in 1948. The former GWR system reluctantly became British Railways Western Region and its metamorphosis during the 1950s coincided with my early trainspotting days around Gloucester. Brand new brown and cream enamel signs adorned the stations and the familiar 'sausage bap-shaped' totem was introduced. The last of these had been removed by BR during the mid-1970s and the early closure of Gotherington meant that it never received them anyway. A little detective work allowed me to discover that the relatively small family firm of Garnier & Son had been awarded the

contract to supply BR with the majority of its original signs.

A visit to a cobbled courtyard in the backstreets of Willesden, North London, found the company still in business, albeit nowadays supplying the highways department with their various road and motorway signage. I eventually persuaded them to manufacture six brown and cream Gotherington totems as a one-off deal for me, using the old BR half-flanged method of fixture. As I write, it is a sobering thought that my totems (gently rusting and fading) have been up on a station longer now than most of the original ones supplied to BR's stations ever were!

It has sometimes been a popular misconception that Western Region stations were painted in the chocolate and cream colours similarly applied to carriages of the Great Western Railway. The reality was a little different, however, as the darker colour was called maroon-brown and not unlike cinnamon in appearance. Original tins of this and other paints were found in the engineer's department at Ashton Gate in Bristol before demolition, and I have matched it almost exactly at Gotherington. Given that paint fades in time, it will always be a talking point in enthusiast circles.

I have not tried to replicate the old Gotherington station, as that clearly would have been impossible for a number of reasons, but back then I seemed to be in the right place at the right time during crucial stages of its development. The overall appearance of the goods shed had been ruined by the addition of some very basic modern glass-panelled patio doors. Presuming that the huge 3-inch-thick sliding doors fitted in 1906 had been lost for ever, I was staggered to discover them by chance in use by a local man as the base for his tractor trailer. Palms were crossed with silver and they are now back where they belong, with a few adaptations.

Above: Mother cleans more bricks in front of the modern patio doors at Gotherington, which were soon replaced by the original GWR ones, which were found on a neighbour's trailer (below).

We are of course not the only people to have purchased a railway station as domestic premises, but my decision to compromise as little as possible has made living here a stark lifestyle choice rather than the demi-paradise imagined by outsiders looking in. It's all incredibly labour intensive. When you are at home on a bitterly cold, rainswept winter's evening arguing about who is going to leave the sofa and make the mammoth trek across the room to nudge up the central heating switch, we may well still be fumbling around on our hands and knees cursing the damp wood that prevents us from coaxing a coal fire into life. Nor is it a place for the faint-hearted to dwell. Our first few summers here were dogged by sleepless nights until we figured out that the deafeningly loud boom that made us sit bolt upright in bed from a deep slumber was generated by the large corrugated-iron roof contracting in the cool night air. We unwittingly added to the timpani section of the alfresco orchestra by fixing large enamel advertising signs to the outside walls. If they would only boom in tune!

Back in 1981, scattered around the former goods yard was a selection of mostly wooden but non-railway-related buildings that we had inherited from the previous owner. Some elderly Sussex fowls tottered around and about, and for a while we bred bantams, but our free-range philosophy was being taken advantage of and it was sometimes weeks before we discovered clutches of eggs. The buildings were swept away when I drew up a rough plan for the yard. A natural pond was created and has attracted a vast array of wildlife, including great crested newts and a 20-foot-long toad!

Admittedly this toad has four large steel wheels and a veranda, but I could not resist bidding for this fine example of the standard GWR brake van ('Toad' being the official railway telegraphic code name for such a vehicle). All the remaining 'Toads' were withdrawn from departmental service on the main railway system in 1984. My example

had been recently serviced at Swindon Works but found itself condemned and dumped in sidings at Barnwood, Gloucester. A kindly shedmaster at Horton Road depot obtained a tender form and advised a bid of around £110, being just above the scrap metal value of the time. Within weeks my new acquisition was on a low-loader weaving its way past the war memorial in our village and negotiating a passage into our yard. Only hours beforehand my uncle and I had hastily laid, by hand, two 20-foot sections of worn-out bullhead rail onto six very rotten sleepers. To this day they continue to support the full 20 tons of my first piece of rolling stock, notwithstanding a list of around 20 degrees to the south…

Since closure in 1949 the goods yard site had returned to nature and frankly looked a bit of a mess. Our quick-fix solution to this was to obtain a pair of goats and train them to eat only railway weeds. They sadly fell short of this remit, regularly devouring large sections of village property, so our flirtation with animal husbandry gained us unwanted celebrity status. 'Plan B' was to reclaim the land in small parcels, beginning with the old signal box site. Also

This page: Our 'Toad' brake van arrives at Gotherington on 6 July 1984 – a heavy creature, this one!

closed and demolished way back in 1949, there was no trace at all of the original box, but a weekend of probing with pick and shovel revealed its solid foundations. Several abortive attempts to acquire a replacement GWR building led me to believe it may be quicker to build one from scratch using original railway materials. The large stones at Withington station were just right for the base of a new structure, so, as the plaintive toll of the church bells echoed in the distance, we sweated and toiled to extract another 200 of these monsters from their lair in the woods. With an average weight of around

a hundredweight each, only 12 at a time could be transported home in my estate car (having first been carried the 75 yards by hand over undulating terrain to reach it). A small GWR lever frame was acquired from the Bristol area and the dismantled wooden remains of a signal cabin from Hampshire were all put together to erect our new box on the old foundations. Regrettably, in our haste to finish the job a miscalculation meant that the pitch of the roof turned out to be slightly too shallow, but in just a few months in the sweltering heat of a late-1980s summer we had constructed a fully fitted new signal box.

Right: The new Gotherington signal box takes shape on 7 June 1989, using stones from Withington station. It is being constructed on the foundations of the original GWR signal box, demolished in 1949.

Sadly the signal box project was to be the last work here that my uncle was involved with, and suddenly the Gotherington workforce was reduced by 50% to just one pair of willing but largely unskilled hands. It quickly became apparent just how utterly essential that help had been over the last eight years when I had been nosing around the old Pengam marshalling yard at Cardiff during its demolition. I had spotted a very large but useful crossing timber that four burly contractors kindly lifted onto the roof-rack of my car. On arrival home, with no help available, it was impossible to remove this tar-soaked trophy on my own. I was therefore forced to set out for work the following morning, in hot sunshine with the tar dripping ever faster onto the roof, windscreen and eventually most of the car bodywork during the course of the day. It was only amusing on reflection, and certainly brought me down to earth with the realisation that if I could not even lift a single large sleeper off the top of my car, then plans to expand the site at Gotherington were ambitious to say the least.

A period of consolidation was enforced upon me as even the maintenance of what had been created so far proved all-consuming. A major crossroads in my life had been reached, as it was very obvious

that without having more time to devote to this enormous project I would lose all that had been achieved so far. Paradoxically, having a very well-paid job had not been an essential element in the story. What had been required was lots of energy and a driving passion for the task in hand.

TREMORS

During the next six years or so we were able to concentrate more on the living quarters of the property, as these had been somewhat ignored due to my minor obsession with the railway side of things. A modern breeze-block interior wall was demolished and the old waiting room re-panelled with tongue-and-groove boards. A shower room was created in the old gents toilet, but we decided to keep visible the period graffiti that had been chiselled into the stone doorway. Just who was 'JA', we wonder? The beautifully proportioned stone-built weigh-house in our yard has been turned into a GWR-style office, complete with wall-mounted gas lamp.

I had often wondered just what sort of sensation the passing of a train would create from inside the house. At precisely 2.47pm on 2 April 1990 there was a bone-shaking rumble and the television set moved 6 inches across the lounge floor… Expecting to see the passing of a massive locomotive outside, I remembered that at that time there were not even any rails laid down. It transpired later that a minor earthquake had occurred locally, and no train has matched that so far!

A few solo field trips were made and I had the chance to take down some of the original Midland Railway iron railings that lined

the track running through Gloucester Park en route to the docks. These now form the backdrop to a small Midland-style platform that I built behind our main shed, to accommodate two large cast-iron lamp standards rescued from Hay-on-Wye station.

On the rare occasions that help was enlisted for a project, it always seemed to result in the accidental spilling of blood and, feeling a little disheartened, I backed off from the creative side of things to do some travelling and rethink a more realistic future plan for

Our original Great Western weigh-house. The metal weighbridge and scales were removed in 1949. The sign on the left speaks for itself!

life at the station. We began to socialise a little more and I liked this renewed freedom that had hitherto been sacrificed due to the huge personal commitment to the work here over the previous decade.

My almost blasé attitude to the whole situation was folly indeed, as gradually even the cycle of maintenance fell way behind schedule.

It was patently obvious that my 'one man band' approach was not going to be viable without complete surrender to the cause, and for the very first time I questioned my motives concerning the Gotherington complex. The solution, once again paradoxically, came out of our temporary hedonistic lifestyle. Some late-night parties proved amusing, such as the discovery of a tramp sleeping on a platform bench at 2.30am. I had heard a noise outside and hastily lit a match to unwittingly illuminate a Fagin-like visage whose body then rose up from the gloom to declare, 'I ain't doin' no 'arm'. To this day I'm not sure who scared who the most, the towering figure in the ragged greatcoat or the cowering individual in the ill-fitting tuxedo.

Another, much less formal, gathering allowed me to meet the man who single-handedly turned around the destiny of Gotherington's future railway history. Not a railway enthusiast as such, but someone with the requisite skills, determination and tools to give a new impetus to the proceedings. Together we were not only to halt the impending decline, but take it far beyond my original expectations.

Above: Removing the Midland Railway railings from the Docks Branch in Gloucester Park, 22 December 1985.

Right: The second platform that Jack and I built was finished in the summer of 1987 and is now used by the Gloucestershire Warwickshire Railway. It now supports a modern waiting shelter constructed by the company in 1987, but my nameboard and original lamp add period ambience.

GOTHERINGTON WEST RISES!

By September 1996 the Gloucestershire Warwickshire Railway (G/WR) had laid enough track to enable its diesel loco No 03069 to run into the platform that we had built for the railway back in 1984, although it would be another nine years before the modern alterations and additions the company made to it allowed passengers to disembark at Gotherington. Being increasingly embarrassed by the stark contrast between our own modern building section and the restored original buildings, ideas were floated about how best to deal with it. As mentioned earlier, we had inherited this new extension from

the previous owner and it forms the core of domestic life here, so demolition was out of the question. Disguise became the preferred option, and a mass of ivy and vines now hides the majority of the reconstituted stone wall on the platform side. My new helper constructed a small canopy over the sealed doorway to give a different perspective and a more railway feel to the scene. A series of rapid professional-looking restoration projects followed and the importance of having someone with a decent tool kit and skill base on site for the first time engendered a more positive attitude in my approach to expansion of the railway scene here.

For a number of years I had been negotiating with the directors of the G/WR with a view to purchasing the old cattle dock adjacent to our property and restoring it to give an insight into the long-lost tradition of moving animals by rail. These structures are extremely rare in preservation, so it was a particularly sad loss when the G/WR finally decided to bulldoze it to oblivion. To try to recompense somewhat for this situation, a decision was taken to wheel out the old cement-mixer again and construct a similar entity on our own land.

As with the two main running platforms, once the blue-brick retaining wall had been built there lay behind a yawning chasm to be

The original 1905-built GWR cattle dock is seen on Christmas Day 1995. This was later bulldozed by the G/WR to make way for its modern signal box.

During construction the cattle dock metamorphosed into more of a general goods loading bay, and we naturally called it Gotherington Goods.

filled. I arranged for several huge lorry-loads of spoil from the demolished Oldacres site (now Tesco) in Bishops Cleeve to be dumped onto our lawn and spent most evenings in the damp autumn air of 1998 laboriously moving it into position by wheelbarrow. I already had on site a couple of short lengths of bullhead rail and the odd wooden sleeper, so to complete the picture we laid some track into it.

It so happened that this new short section of railway appeared to be on the same alignment as the original single siding put down by the Great Western Railway in 1906, and removed in 1949. Plenty of dark grey large-format ballast came to light to verify this, and we collected enough to box in our new railhead, which lay in splendid isolation, just 200 yards from the G/WR main running line.

The glorious prospect of maybe linking up to a real working railway line seemed too good to miss, and I formulated a plan of action that I thought could achieve this and, by doing so, give the G/WR an option for future events. In the G/WR yard at Winchcombe lay the twisted and rotting remains of a genuine GWR pagoda-style

Right: The mangled remains of the 'Pagoda' shelter arrive on site on 10 November 1999.

waiting shelter, which had been rescued some years ago from Willersey station and was now sadly neglected and in need of significant, time-consuming restoration work. My man with the tools was 'champing at the bit' for this one, and it became possible to exchange money in return for the remaining rusted corrugated-iron portions to be brought to Gotherington yard.

Things really came together quickly now as I also purchased from the railway what was once the run-round loop at Far Stanley and had been left in situ but disconnected. The bullhead rail, in various lengths, together

with around 200 wooden sleepers of variable quality, were dismantled and dragged along to Gotherington in the first week of December 1999. My plan was to recreate a little cameo scene from GWR history that the public passenger-carrying preservation groups are not permitted to do under current Health & Safety regulations. During the Edwardian period the GWR experimented with railmotors, i.e. a single carriage with integral boiler and drive mechanism. A number of small halts were constructed using timber for the platform and usually a classic oriental-style corrugated 'Pagoda' waiting shelter on top. Being a private

concern we could ignore the HSE ruling and replicate such a scene very accurately indeed. Three stations on the Honeybourne line sported this style of structure, so old photographs of Gretton, Laverton and, of course, Willersey were studied closely before starting work.

A single wooden railway sleeper is approximately 8ft 6in long, 10 inches wide, 5 inches deep and is very, very heavy. Thirty-five of these hefty beasts were physically man-handled into position and bolted together to provide a base for our 'Pagoda' shelter to sit upon. The shelter's mangled pieces were then laid out in the yard and for a while it seemed that we had taken delivery of little more than a pile of holes held together by some bits of rusted corrugated iron. A rapid programme of surgery ensued, and within a couple of weeks my man with a grinder had replaced all of the rotten sections, beaten the battered apex back into shape and made new finials for the roof. New lead flashing was purchased to replace the distorted strips of tinplate resting on each corner and, when gently beaten, followed the graceful curves of the oriental roof design. Almost all of the original angle iron internal support structure was beyond salvage, but its replacement, although rather costly, bore the same steelmaker's trade markings. In excess of 400 holes had to be painstakingly drilled before the constituent parts could be bolted together

Above left: Will the grinder at work restoring the damaged 'Pagoda' roof on 7 January 2000.

Above: Will uses our borrowed generator to power his jigsaw. The rain does not stop us piecing together the timber platform on 5 September 2000.

and fixed onto the wooden base, which sat about 4 feet above ground level. Another 41 sleepers were then cut and lap-jointed together to create a 70-foot-long platform support, upon which were laid a number of chunky, well-seasoned planks. After adding typical post-and-wire fencing, a pair of hand-made oil lamps and a nameboard, it was decided that the name 'Gotherington West' (being geographically correct) would sound quite authentic.

We now had to connect Gotherington West with Gotherington Goods, which lay 200 yards away, so during a five-day period in mid-August 2000 a total of 157 chaired wooden sleepers were dragged manually into position. This was a back-breaking two-man operation using the cutting edge of 19th-century technology, viz a piece of apparatus known as sleeper nips. These may appear familiar to those avid readers of the works of the Marquis de Sade, and I can assure you that in the hands of a novice they can give both pain and pleasure in equal amounts. Bullhead rail of various lengths was then dropped into the chairs, at first using just the two-man-operated nips; however, common sense later prevailed and a JCB was hired to finish the

job. A splendid GWR-style wooden crossing gate was made from scratch in our workshop (the third such gate built by the grinding man), intended to allow access for trains from the G/WR line at some stage in the future. Sadly this will not now be possible as that organisation has built its modern non-authentic signal building far too close to our gate.

No railway restoration project would be complete without a telegraph pole or two, so four of these 25-foot-high columns were bear-hugged into their respective holes and each fitted out with genuine porcelain insulators.

Below: This sleeper-built structure, seen on 19 February 2000, will support the restored 'Pagoda' building and eventually become Gotherington West Halt.

Left: More grinding on the metalwork of the 'Pagoda', which is now in position on its sleeper-built base.

Below: Sixty-four half-lap joints were hand cut into the old sleepers to form the single-coach-length platform in true GWR railmotor style. This 29 August 2000 view shows what the junction with the Gloucestershire Warwickshire Railway would have looked like had it wished to join up with us.

To complete the picture I ordered 40 tons of ballast from St Briavels quarry in the Forest of Dean, then, using just a wheelbarrow and shovel, I single-handedly moved every last nugget of it onto our trackbed from the enormous piles dumped by the lorries in our yard.

From the day that the remaining pieces of the 'Pagoda' arrived on site to the final painting and application of creosote to the finished platform amounted to 1,200 man-hours of work over an 18-month period by just two people. We now had in effect our own private standard gauge railway with boarding facilities at either end, and in 2001 Gotherington West won the Ian Allan-sponsored National Railway Heritage award.

Left: A lamp hand-made by Will.

Below: Gotherington West Halt on 14 December 2001, complete with hand-made lamps, nameboard, wicket gate and level crossing gate.

MOTIVE POWER ARRIVES

The humble but ubiquitous platelayers' hut was designed to offer cheap shelter for track maintenance gangs, and when we moved to Gotherington in 1981 examples remained at Far Stanley, Winchcombe and Stanway. Now only the shell of the latter remains, so we resolved to slot another missing piece into our railway jigsaw and construct an example for our line. The basic design principle for GWR huts varied little, so first of all a staggered red-brick chimney breast was built before stacking 30 wooden sleepers upright in the ground (more bear-hugging) to form the walls of the building. Planks around 3 inches thick were used for a door and sloping roof, then gaps between the sleeper walls were stuffed with newspapers. Once the coal fire is lit and the tar starts oozing from the timbers you have the perfect ambience for railway life in the steam age.

Of course once people get to know that you have built a railway line in your back yard, their expectation that a locomotive will follow could be forgiven. The reality is, however, that a working steam locomotive could be a liability in private ownership, requiring skills I do not possess and accruing bills I would not be prepared to pay. However, there seemed very little point in building a standard gauge railway from scratch without adding some form of motive power, so a realistic option for our short length of permanent way was sought out.

The GWR had experimented with small petrol-engined locomotives from as early as 1923 for works yards where the use of a coal-fired engine was deemed hazardous or uneconomic. This continued into the early years of British Railways when a batch of 12 tiny vehicles were constructed by Messrs Wickham of Ware for use as inspection trolleys. The two-seater machines resembled a toy car on rails and were originally fitted with the notoriously recalcitrant JAP engine. Only a few remain and I purchased the heavily stripped shell of one such vehicle, which arrived on site in March 2002. Just two months later my man with the grinder had hand-built a totally new

The finished platelayers' hut on the approach to Gotherington Goods on 15 July 2003.

back end and exhaust system for it. Once the new windscreen, hand-sewn hood, scratch-built headlamps and refurbished seats were fitted it was time to look under the bonnet.

A rare 1961 DAF 'variomatic' car engine had been installed at some point, and exploded into life like a Gatling machine gun before catching fire one rainy Sunday afternoon as we ran parallel to a train on the adjacent G/WR line. Spares were sought and found locally, so occasionally

Above: The derelict Wickham trolley on 12 March 2002.

Right: The completely refurbished Wickham trolley in its original BR guise as PWM 2779. It is sitting on the turntable outside its purpose-built shed on 8 April 2003.

Far right: The newly fabricated back end alongside the old on 26 July 2002.

our mean maroon machine is available for rides and anyone brave enough to stay the distance will not forget the experience. A purpose-built shed was erected to house the Wickham; as was normal practice, it stands at right angles to our running line. Visitors are always amused when I single-handedly put the vehicle to bed by laying down a metal H-frame, then pushing the vehicle onto this and pivoting the whole thing through 90 degrees before allowing the Wickham to roll gently into the shed. The whole ingenious process can take less than 1 minute flat.

No self-respecting railway goods yard would have been complete without a loading gauge to monitor the height of laden wagons leaving for travel on the main line. I had already rescued an original metal hoop, and fabrication of the early 'gallows' style was favoured. In just six working days from the delivery of the timber it stood erect, casting an ominous shadow over Gotherington yard.

When the G/WR started running its trains to Gotherington in 1997, I began to be aware that some of my 'collection' looked rather incongruous in such close proximity. The main culprit seemed to be an ex-Southern Railway signal that had rather dominated the skyline here since planted in 1988. Coming originally from the Lymington branch in Hampshire, it has now been collected by an enthusiast and taken

to a more appropriate home. We had been able to operate this signal from our own signal box, and its removal left us with one less toy to play with, so a decision was taken to erect a typical early wooden GWR example, adjacent to our own running line. I already had enough metal fittings to make up a lower-quadrant semaphore, but no post, so a beautifully tapered piece of cedar wood was obtained.

The grinding man then spent hours and hours painting and sanding until the finished product resembled a huge piece of white porcelain pointing skywards. It was all very smart and authentic, but sited too far away from our signal box to be operated in a safe and practical manner, so a small ground frame hut was built from scratch to house new operating levers. Some battered but sturdy Colombian

pine timbers were rescued from a bonfire in Winchcombe yard when the G/WR decided to burn the remains of Stratford-upon-Avon East signal box; now nicely tidied up, these form the bulk of the framework for our Gotherington West Ground Frame building.

I have always been anxious to avoid the Gotherington West project looking like a museum, and as the intention was to try to

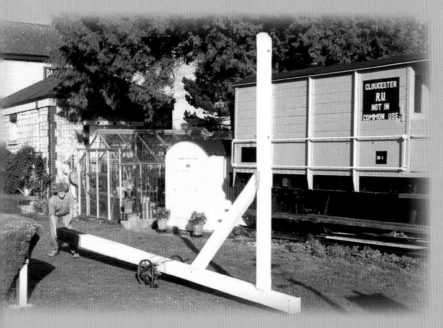

Above: The loading gauge is moved from our workshop...

Right: ...to its place on the branch, 31 August 2004.

replicate a typical ex-GWR country branch line, I now declare the job finished. Further additions I feel would be superfluous. The huge programme of maintenance that lies ahead with so much wood, hardly protected at all by today's modern paints, doesn't bear thinking about, but suffice to say that we will stay true to the cause and not take the easy options favoured by others when trying to depict authentic railway history.

FULL STEAM AHEAD!

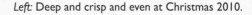

This was supposed to be the end of the tale, but events occurring in 2010 have produced the definitive chapter in the story of our time at Gotherington. The well-documented landslip on the Gloucestershire Warwickshire line, just to the south of us, necessitated all trains terminating in the main platform, and this was to be the limit of operation during the huge GW175 gala celebrations. A phone call from the newly reshuffled boardroom of the G/WR

Left: Deep and crisp and even at Christmas 2010.

Below: Steam age smoulderings, May 2010.

asked us if we would like to participate in this event by opening up our land and running line to the general public for the very first time. We were more than happy to oblige, especially as arrangements were to be made for a small steam locomotive from the Gwili Railway to give rides in an adapted brake van. Not since 1949, when the line was lifted by BR, had a steam locomotive entered Gotherington goods yard, and never in such an unorthodox manner as the arrival of this little engine, which had to be painstakingly jacked sideways from the main running line onto our isolated 'branch'. This process took many hours of skilful manoeuvring and shouting.

Having agreed to allow the general public into our back garden, we now had to consider the implications. For nearly 30 years it had been a playground for big boys (and a few brave girls), but could now be viewed as a potential danger zone for young families. The Railway Inspector had insisted on security fencing along the length of our running line, but visitors were ushered over from trains arriving from Toddington and boarded 'our'

Right: From a greenfield site to a public passenger-carrying railway – this is 0-4-0 saddle tank RSH 7058 masquerading as BR No 1144 running between Gotherington Goods and Gotherington West platforms on 5 June 2010.

Opposite: Little Gotherington is an area created to display former Southern Railway items, but now includes some recovered edging slabs from Tewkesbury station.

train at Gotherington Goods bay for the ride to Gotherington West and return. The wooden platform at Gotherington West had more movement than a bouncy castle; the derelict bull cart had more shards of metal protruding from it than Boadicea's chariot, and our signal box steps had rotted, but nobody fell into the

pond and we raised a substantial amount of money for the three charities that the G/WR chose to support.

Further stories of the Gotherington restoration adventures can be found in back issues of the G/WR's house magazine, 'The Cornishman'.

HIDDEN CORNERS

SOUTHERN RAILWAY
WARNING

— **WARNING** —
STOP LOOK & LISTEN
BEFORE CROSSING THE LINE.

LITTLE GOTHERINGTON

This page: What was once just a massive bramble patch has been landscaped using original railway artefacts. The rather regal-looking seat was sculpted by Will from the large slate slabs that formed the gents urinal at Barbers Bridge station near Newent in Gloucestershire. The bird bath seen on the left I made using a large amount of metal washers from the undersides of railway sleepers.

THE WORKSHOP

Above: Hand-made GWR-style platform lamps are in various stages of construction.

Far left: Repairs to barrows from Cheltenham Lansdown station and Gloucester goods yard.

Left: Yet another brand new level crossing gate is built from scratch.

Left: Restoring the platform trolley retrieved from a Gwent scrapyard in 1983. The large wooden sign came from the branch leading to the Emlyn Foundry at Gloucester. Railway wagons would be shunted to the furnace by a road tractor adapted for the purpose.

Below: A brand-new GWR-style wheelbarrow was fashioned around an original wheel unearthed from excavations of a local navvies' encampment.

Where did that come from?

Platform bricks and edging stones
Withington
Pontypool Crane Street
Bourton-on-the-Water

Spear-head railings
Ross-on-Wye
Gloucester Docks branch

Nameboard posts
Llangennech
Llangeinor
Cheltenham Malvern Road

Cast-iron lamp standards
Ninian Park Halt, Cardiff (3)
Ross-on-Wye
Brynmenyn (2)
Over Junction, Gloucester (2)
Pontypool Crane Street (2)
Undy (2)
Hay-on-Wye (2)
Ammanford
Merthyr goods yard
Sharpness

Platform barrows
Gloucester goods depot
Cheltenham Lansdown station

Platform benches
Pantyffynon
Nant-y-Bwch
Bransford Road
Crumlin

Platform trolleys
Shrewsbury
Droitwich Spa
Kemble
Gloucester Eastgate

Poster boards
Malvern
Merthyr Vale

Fire buckets
Basseleg
Rhymney

Fire alarm, cabinet, axes, notices etc
Gloucester Central station

Gates
Withington
Barbers Bridge
Gretton
Gloucester
Panteg & Griffithstown

Right: Garden machinery! The first steam on our private line, May 2010.

Gents urinal
Barbers Bridge

Enamel signs
Honeybourne
Droitwich Spa

Lamp hut
Barnwood, Gloucester

'Pagoda' shelter
Willersey

Signal box
Eastleigh
Withington

Southern Railway signal
Lymington Town

Together with items from
Bromsgrove
Soudley
Boncath

...and many other locations

This page: Our own individual web site!

PAST and PRESENT

Right: Both platforms at Gotherington had been demolished, as seen on 21 September 1981…

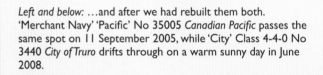

Left and below: …and after we had rebuilt them both. 'Merchant Navy' 'Pacific' No 35005 *Canadian Pacific* passes the same spot on 11 September 2005, while 'City' Class 4-4-0 No 3440 *City of Truro* drifts through on a warm sunny day in June 2008.

Main picture: This is the view from the up platform, which we had just finished building, on 17 November 1984. The down platform has yet to be constructed.

Right: Seen from more or less the same spot, with the down platform now finished, is 'Merchant Navy' 'Pacific' No 35005 *Canadian Pacific*.

Left: Savita digs out the footings for the new down platform on 20 April 1986.

PLATFORM FOR
STRATFORD · UPON · AVON
LEAMINGTON SPA
BIRMINGHAM (SNOW HILL) AND
CHELTENHAM SPA (ST JAMES)

Right: Gotherington West Halt was built on this site by just two people. The main station building can be seen on the right.

Below: The finished halt is seen from more or less the same viewpoint on 5 May 2006.

Above: Gotherington goats on Christmas Day 1987.

Below: In exactly the same spot in December 2004 we find our Wickham trolley awaiting the 'right away'

Below: 'Views from the main line.'